About the Author

Joe Castello was born in 1939. He graduated in Pharmacy and then created a small chain of pharmacies. He is now part of a family business that is focused on bars and restaurants.
He was active in rugby, judo and skiing until commonsense prevailed. He still plays in a 9-piece jazz and blues band.

Dedication

This book is dedicated to those who give total commitment to the road for recovery. It takes great courage and perseverance to continue the program, day after day.
The dedication also needs to be shared with those who give the love, support and encouragement to those who travel.

Joe Castello

The Joe Public Guide To Addiction
(An Aid For Parents)

PUBLISHERS LTD.

Copyright © Joe Castello (2015)

The right of Joe Castello to be identified as author of this work has been asserted by him in accordance with section 77 and 78 of the Copyright, Designs and Patents Act 1988.

All rights reserved. No part of this publication may be reproduced, stored in a retrieval system, or transmitted in any form or by any means, electronic, mechanical, photocopying, recording, or otherwise, without the prior permission of the publishers.

Any person who commits any unauthorized act in relation to this publication may be liable to criminal prosecution and civil claims for damages.

A CIP catalogue record for this title is available from the British Library.

ISBN 978 1 78455 257 2

www.austinmacauley.com

First Published (2015)
Austin Macauley Publishers Ltd.
25 Canada Square
Canary Wharf
London
E14 5LB

Printed and bound in Great Britain

Acknowledgments

My sincere thanks to James Wells for kindly donating the cover design.

www.jameswellsgraphics.com

INTRODUCTION

This guide was written by the parent of an addict, who hoped that as a by-product, the exercise would prove to be cathartic.

Its primary purpose however, is to help other parents who are faced with the pain and anguish of this all too common problem.

I fully realise that every case of addiction is different, but without doubt, common patterns frequently emerge.

Every parent wants to proactively help their child recover from this condition, but often find it difficult to find clear advice as to how they can help. This publication is intended to act as a sort of road map which will help them to navigate some of the problems they may encounter.

If knew then what I know now, I am convinced that my son's recovery would have begun much sooner, and would have probably been more successful. I freely admit to my long lasting ignorance of addiction, and to my slow learning curve that would have better equipped me to be of greater help.

Like it or not, as a parent, we ARE deeply involved in our child's journey to recovery (regardless of their age) -- if for no other reason than the fact that their health and happiness problems impinge heavily on our own health and happiness.

We love them unconditionally, but they frequently exasperate and anger us when they fail to take our common sense advice, and fail to show any glimmer of an instinct for self-survival.

Whilst reading this publication, please always try to remember that an addict never "chooses" to be an addict, any more than anyone would choose to be diabetic, epileptic or physically disabled.

Nobody who flirts with a recreational drug, and this includes alcohol, expects that particular drug to eventually control and then to ruin their lives!!

The summary that follows is intended to be objective.

The contents that follow the summary however, will inevitably be rather more subjective because they represent my experience.

I would like to thank those addicts and parents of addicts who I consulted about this publication. Their helpful feedback enabled me to make a few valuable changes to the final text.

Finally I would like to thank my son, who after reading the final draft gave it his ringing endorsement.

Without his unhesitating approval I would not have proceeded to publication.

This title, together with others in The Joe Public Guide series, is available via
www.joepublicguide.com

SUMMARY

1. Diagnose that there is a possible problem, because of irrational behaviour patterns and feedback from friends.

2. Confront the addict regarding their addiction, and be prepared for their denial.

3. Understand that addiction is a disease.

4. Look for unreliability, lies, stealing habits, financial problems and financial chaos.

5. Never give CASH to an addict, regardless of how plausible the request. Don't pay their debts for them, and allow their finances to go into free-fall.

6. Allow them to hit rock bottom.

7. Encourage them to admit to their addiction because without this admission they cannot start the journey of recovery.

8. Encourage them to go into re-hab, where they will learn that they have a disease. It is essential that they pay for it themselves if they have the resources. People are much more inclined to heed advice if they have paid for it!

9. Persuade them that attending self-help meetings and participating in the "12 steps" program is an essential part of their journey of recovery.

10. Understand that their journey of recovery is a lifetime journey, and that they will NEVER be free of addiction. All that we can hope for is that they successfully manage it.

11. Understand that they may well repeatedly relapse and return to rock bottom before the journey re-starts again.

12. Learn how to manage your relationship with your addict.

13. Remember that nobody chooses to be an addict, any more than they would chose to be diabetic, epileptic or physically disabled.

14. Encourage them to begin a new lifestyle with new friends in a healthy environment.

15. Encourage them to consider Cognitive Behavioural Therapy (CBT) which they also need to pay for themselves if they have the resources.

16. Persuade them to study The Art of Happiness by the Dalai Lama.

17. Epilogue. Be aware that despite their best efforts, a successful recovery eludes some addicts. We as family have to steel ourselves to the reality that continuing and chronic addiction often causes death.

18. The Premiere League of Dangerous Drugs.

1. Diagnose that there is a possible problem, because of irrational behaviour patterns and feedback from friends

There is an old saying which I regard to be a truism:

"Show me the 7-year-old, and I'll show you the man".

In order to try to understand your addict as an adult, cast your mind back to their characteristics when they were 7 years of age.

I clearly remember mine as a child who was:

- Very contented and able to amuse himself for hours.
- Very placid and with no temper tantrums.
- Very open in his affections.
- Very sociable.

This is the person that I am always looking for, and who I hope to help separate from "the addict" that is a parasite on his life, on our relationship and on all our lives.

During the addiction years, we all witnessed a change of character, which made him both unreliable and untrustworthy. Because this happened over a period of time, and because he was a mature adult of 30 years, we drifted into denial.

This denial was steadfastly maintained, even though close friends were confirming our observations and openly suggesting his excessive drug use. This feedback was well intentioned, but we retained our stance of denial.

Looking back, this may have been because:

- We knew that his generation were known as the "chemical generation", and that they were epidemically experimenting with drugs.
- We didn't clearly understand the difference between enthusiastic recreational use and addiction.
- We felt that we had little influence over the lifestyle of a 30 year old.
- We rather stupidly thought that things would change for the better once the experimentation was finished.
- We didn't know how to deal with the reality of addiction.

Many addicts tend to be People-Pleasers, who because of their reluctance to say "no", surrender considerable power from their own lives. In order to be a People-Pleaser, it is usually necessary to become an habitual liar. Addicts who wish to recover will need to learn to assert their own rights and not to feel apologetic about it.

The irrational behaviour of an addict will be compounded if they suffer from a mental health problem such as clinical depression or are bi-polar. If a professional diagnosis proves this to be the case, the mental health problem obviously needs separate treatment. This would not however lessen the advice given to help the addiction problem.

2. Confront the addict regarding their addiction, and be prepared for their denial

Whenever we did confront our son about "drugs", he never denied occasionally using them, but he always denied that there was a problem.

I need to point out that I had always taken a firm stance against hard drugs, and even when they were in their 20s, I had written a letter to both my sons articulating the problems associated with hard drugs. This was prompted by my considerable pharmaceutical experience, and by the fact that we had taken our family business into the leisure trade, together with all of its inherent temptations.

For the record, I have always been a moderate drinker, although I didn't warn my sons of the possible problems that could stem from alcohol. I now reflect that I was far too liberal in my attitude to alcohol, which was probably encouraged by my love affair with the game of rugby football and the social life that goes with it. Both of my sons also fell in love with the game. One was not readily attracted to alcohol, whereas the other one took to it "like a duck to water" --- you can guess which one!

I have used marijuana, but failed to strike up a sustainable relationship with it. I have never encouraged its use because I had generally observed that although it never stifled dreams, it did seem to stifle achievement.

I have twice used cocaine whilst abroad, but failed to be impressed. I naively thought that addiction could only develop from heavy use. Subsequent to that experimentation, and in about 2010, Dr. Antonello Bonci of the University of California established that taking cocaine even ONCE can trigger addiction. Although the odds might be low, on reflection I now realise that I was lucky!!

Although I confronted my son on numerous occasions about drug use and its dangers, he continued for years to be in denial. Looking back with hindsight, his denial became greater as his addiction became more established.

3. Understand that addiction is a disease

As previously stated, no-one chooses to be an addict, any more than they would choose to be diabetic, epileptic, or physically disabled.

A great deal of work has been done on this subject, and the findings are accepted by the majority of the medical fraternity.

In summary, most definitions of disease easily accommodate addiction as a disease. This position has been confirmed by clinical experience, scientific experiment, and legal precedent. It is to be hoped that with continued research and accumulated knowledge, the true nature of the disease of addiction will emerge with even more precision.

Drug addiction is a disease in which:

- The drug acts as the cause of the problem.

- There is a loss of control over the drug use behaviour, once usage has been started.
- The addict craves for their drug of choice, and needs that drug, both in larger amounts and in greater frequency.
- The drug creates a physical allergy in those who are destined to become addicts, as opposed to those who continue to be recreational users. Some people can drink and they are fine, whereas some people drink, are possessed by booze, and drink themselves to death.
- There is substantial evidence that addiction is genetically transmitted. If a person has a grandparent that is an addict, there is a 4 times greater chance that they will be an addict. If both parents are addicted, the chances are 8 times greater.
- Addiction is a disease of the primitive midbrain which involves relapse and requires a lifetime strategy of ongoing practice and care.
- Total abstinence is the only effective cure.

Data tells us that if a young person can make it to adulthood (say 21) without using alcohol, drugs or tobacco, the chances of their becoming dependent is virtually nil—or if not nil, greatly decreased.

A lot of people move through these years, experimenting, partying, and in some cases abusing, but they don't get hooked. They stop altogether, or they moderate their behaviour to a social norm. It's therefore obvious that if a youngster keeps totally clean during these formative years, the risk of addiction is greatly reduced.

4. Look for unreliability, lies, stealing habits, financial problems and financial chaos

Uncontrollable craving for the drug of choice, and the behaviours that accompany these overpowering cravings, include:

- Lying.
- Stealing.
- Radical negative personality changes.
- Withdrawal from formally important relationships into a rather reclusive nature.

Drug cravings become an absolute priority, and hence a previously honest person feels driven to lie, steal and cheat, in order to fund their habit.

It is therefore no surprise that a huge percentage of our prison population are drug addicts or drug dealers.

In the brain of the addict, addictive cravings are equated with survival—not pleasure, not fun, but survival. These cravings become more powerful than the instinct for life itself.

Under these circumstances, it is no surprise that the moral compass of the addict becomes totally disorientated.

My son had never been materialistic, and was therefore not too respectful of money. This was accompanied by his very casual approach to life and a lack of appetite for responsibility. He had breezed through life by using his considerable charm and remarkable inter-personal skills, to compensate for his lack of organisation.

Actions speak louder than words, and I was slow to learn that he often manipulated me so that I didn't "follow the money". If I had stood back and ruthlessly followed his net cash position, I would have learned sooner that my son had considerable problems. An addict will always be skint!

5. Never give CASH to an addict, regardless of how plausible the request. Don't pay their debts for them, and allow their finances to go into free-fall

We have established that we must not subsidise them for the good things in life because this money will always be diverted and converted into drugs. As parents we have been driven to distraction by the way our "help" has been used for drugs, and how over a period of time all of my son's own assets have been squandered on self-destruction.

Even though I was keeping a journal of this painful journey, as loving parents it was too easy to take pity on his plight and to ease his discomfort with cash.

For a considerable time we were often settling many of his bad debts because we felt his personal behaviour was damaging the family reputation in which we have considerable pride. Our actions concealed the reality of his financial predicament.

After many years of getting it wrong, I am now convinced that the way to help your addict is by either feeding them, or giving them actual food --- but NEVER by giving cash. Giving cash merely "enables" them to buy their drug of choice. It follows that paying their debts slows down the "free-fall" and is another form of "enabling".

6. Allow them to hit rock bottom

It is really hard on the parents to witness their child (regardless of age) descending to rock bottom, and even harder to play a part in accelerating this process. Such actions run totally against parental instinct.

We simply have to deny them cash so that we don't "enable" them. The consequence of this as previously stated, is their faster journey to the bottom.

In my case, my son got to the point where he had no employment, had sold his house and spent the equity on drugs, had no car, no TV and zero cash. What he did have were a number of debts. It was only then, that he tearfully asked for help, and admitted that he couldn't continue to live the life that he was suffering.

Until this admission of a problem happens, the journey of recovery cannot begin. It is essential that the addict becomes fully motivated to get clean, and becomes the driving force for this process and for this journey. ALL treatment is a waste of time and resource unless the addict admits to their addiction, and cries out for help.

7. Encourage them to admit to their addiction so that they can start the journey to recovery

By not "enabling" them, you allow them to hit rock bottom sooner rather than later.

I realise that I repeat some of this text, but the repetition is an intentional way of emphasising some of the more important points.

It's not until they hit rock bottom that you will hear the cry for help, which acts as the starting gun for the road to recovery.

They need to admit that they have a problem, and then to articulate that they want to do something about it.

When these things happen, you feel that both they and you have made a quantum leap forward.

It isn't the end of the problem, but we can feel optimistic that it is the "beginning of the end" of the problem.

It is most important that the addict identifies the substance that they are abusing. This is because some substances such as opiates, cause a physical addiction which will require the use of methadone, whereas substances such as cocaine create a mental/emotional addiction.

8. Encourage them to go into re-hab, where they will learn that they have a disease. It is essential that they pay for it themselves if they have the resources. People are much more inclined to heed advice if they have paid for it!

My initial opposition to re-hab as a self-indulgent soft option was based on ignorance. I'm sure there are some clinics where profits come before people, but I have no doubt whatsoever that the voluntary entry into re-hab is an essential part of the journey of recovery.

Addicts are initially helped to understand that they have a disease, not a moral failure or a lack of will. It is imperative that they understand this concept.

When we use the word "drug", this means the drug of choice and obviously includes alcohol.

The nature of addiction is illustrated by the preoccupation with acquiring the drug despite the adverse consequences, and a pattern of relapse despite those additional consequences.

A drug user cannot stop using their drug of choice, once they have started, because they have no control.

For the alcoholic, 1 drink is too many, but 10 drinks is not enough!!

The loss of control over the drug, once established, exists for the user's lifetime and destructively affects his or her life.

The effects include disruptions to relationships, employment, personal finances, as well as a steady but continuous decline in physical and mental health. Addiction to drugs is a morbid process. Simply put, it will cause the addict's death if untreated.

The proven successful program that has helped millions of addicts achieve recovery, is a set of principles referred to as the 12 steps.

It is to this program that the addicts are introduced in re-hab.

The 1st step gets the addict to admit that they are powerless over their drug, and that their lives had become unmanageable.

It is the loss of control that is central to the definition of addiction as a disease. For addicts to begin the journey to recovery, they must confront the reality of this loss of control. To attempt the use of willpower after drug usage has started is simply not an option.

In fact, a common reason for addicts to relapse is because of their inability or unwillingness to accept this fundamental aspect of the disease.

Without accepting the loss of control an addict may relapse anytime between a few days to many years. This relapse can still occur even if they have committed themselves to a program of TOTAL abstinence from ALL drugs, regardless of the one that they are addicted to.

The addict is definitely powerless over their drug, but NOT powerless over their addiction. It's like having a normal clean life on one riverbank and a life of addiction on the other. In so much as the addict has to cross over the bridge to start using drugs, they have power over their addiction by refusing to make the crossing.

Recovery from the disease of addiction relies heavily on the addict taking personal responsibility for adhering to the 12 steps program!

It is important to note that the addict's responsibility extends only up to a well defined line: the pledge not to take the FIRST drink or drug.

If the pledge is broken, he or she has then lost control of the drug.

This new responsibility therefore calls for TOTAL abstinence which amounts to a total voluntary remake of lifestyle. This control of lifestyle and attitudes demonstrates the addict's TOTAL control over the addiction.

It also demonstrates that the loss of control referred to, was solely because of a vulnerability to a chemical.

Since total abstinence involves giving up both drink and drugs, the addict sometimes finds this difficult to explain to the world in which they socialise. They need to find a way to present this, which closes off the need for further discussion.

An important aspect of re-hab is for the addict to learn how to set objectives and how to develop coping mechanisms which prevent relapse.

Without proper treatment, the addict is often helpless against the disease, just as the person who dies of untreated hypertension. Both people should be offered treatment and an opportunity to mend their ways.

Addicts are not responsible for being genetically vulnerable to addiction. Yet they are responsible for their disease, if we take "responsibility" to mean acceptance that the disease exists, and that the addict is responsible for a change in lifestyle.

One addict described the problem thus: "I feel as if there is a trap-door in my head, and that when opened up, it looks like the driving cab of a bus. There is a large steering wheel and a large leather seat etc. The problem is, I have an addict driving my bus! I need to fight that addict for control so that I can be the driver of my own bus!!! As a parent, I am happy to help fight that addict, to recover the steering wheel, drive a few miles, and then very willingly hand the wheel back to my son.

The 12 steps are a powerful statement of personal responsibility.

It needs restating that this program has guided millions of addicts to recovery.

If the addict has no resources to pay for their re-hab, one option is for the parents to pay and for this payment to be regarded as part of their inheritance in advance. This strategy may remove any friction between siblings. If there are no family resources to pay for re-hab, there is a strong body of opinion that suggests that The State should bear the cost. The argument being that the sooner an addict becomes clean, the sooner that they are no longer a liability to The State in many possible ways (health, crime, welfare support, etc.). I personally have started to lobby my MP to this effect.

9. Persuade them that attending self-help meetings and participating in the "12 steps" program is an essential part of their journey to recovery

I make no apology for labouring the importance of the "12 step" program which originally comes from The Big Book and which was written in 1939 for the benefit of alcoholics. It has been the foundation stone for the successful recovery of millions. It is still read by addicts of every type and is regarded as a bible for addiction.

Here are the 12 steps as written in 1939. I must emphasise however that there are also SECULAR VERSIONS now available for those who are not comfortable with the religious flavour of the original:

1. We admitted that we were powerless over alcohol, and that our lives had become unmanageable.
2. We came to believe that a power greater than ourselves could restore us to sanity.
3. We made a decision to turn our will and our lives over to God as we understood him.
4. We made a searching and fearless moral inventory of ourselves.
5. We admitted to God, ourselves and another human being, the exact nature of our wrongs.
6. We were entirely ready to have God remove all these defects of character.
7. We humbly asked Him to remove our shortcomings.
8. We made a list of all persons we had harmed, and became willing to make amends to them all.
9. We made direct amends to such people wherever possible, except when to do so would injure them and others.
10. We continued to take personal inventory and when we were wrong promptly admitted it.
11. We sought through prayer and meditation to improve our conscious contact with God, as we understood Him, praying only for knowledge of His will for us and the power to carry that out.
12. Having had a spiritual awakening as a result of these Steps, we tried to carry this message to alcoholics, and to practice the principles in all our affaires.

Running in conjunction with these 12 Steps are 12 Promises which need to be fulfilled by those who participate. The fulfilment may be quickly achieved or may be slowly achieved, but these promises are all achievable by hard work.

The 12 promises are:

1. If we are painstaking about this phase of our development, we will be amazed before we are half way through the program.
2. We are going to know a new freedom and a new happiness.
3. We will not regret the past or wish to shut the door on it.
4. We will comprehend the word serenity and we will know peace.
5. No matter how far down the scale we have gone, we will see how our experience can benefit others.
6. The feelings of uselessness and self-pity will disappear.
7. We will lose interest in selfish things and gain interest in our fellows.
8. Self-seeking will slip away.
9. Our whole attitude and outlook on life will change.
10. Fear of people and economic insecurity will leave us.
11. We will intuitively know how to handle situations which use to baffle us.
12. We will suddenly realise that God is doing for us what we could not do for ourselves.

PLEASE NOTE that there are SECULAR versions of this text.

10. Understand that their journey of recovery is a lifetime journey, and that they will NEVER be free of addiction. All we can hope for is that they successfully manage it

Not much can be added to this. It's a fact!! --- just as night follows day!

As the diabetic and the person with chronic hypertension need to manage their conditions, or face the harsh consequences, so does the addict.

11. Understand that they may well repeatedly relapse and return to rock bottom before the journey re-starts again

We have already stated the route of recovery from addiction.

What the addict needs to do is:

- Enter the 12 step program with commitment.
- Attend meetings as suggested.
- Become totally abstinent from all drink and drugs.

If it's that simple, why do people relapse? --- and yet they do!

Nobody chooses to relapse, because when they do, it emphasises the pain, loneliness, and despair of addiction.

It means they have failed, and nobody enjoys failure.

Total abstinence from all drugs is the only way to overcome addiction. However, whilst abstinence is the beginning, the only hope for recovery is if it is accompanied by a profound emotional and spiritual change.

The process of recovery isn't easy. It takes great courage and perseverance to continue the program for recovery, day after day.

Part of the recovery process is to move forward in spite of whatever personal problems may stand in the way.

It needs to be both remembered and understood that long-lasting progress in recovery happens slowly, and may well need the addict to return time and time again to the 1st Step. Victory is only possible if the addict totally surrenders to the fact that they have no control whatsoever over their drug of choice.

Even long periods of abstinence do not guarantee continued freedom from the pain and trouble that addiction can bring. This was graphically illustrated by the high profile death of Eva Rausing, who after 11 years of being clean, lapsed into alcohol in order to celebrate the new millennium. Her decline and death in 2012 were precipitated by her relapse.

The emptiness and despair suffered by the relapsed addict can only be filled by total commitment to the 12 Step program. It is here that the addiction is addressed in all its complexity, by this simple program.

There is a deeply spiritual nature to the program, and this spiritual awakening is an important aspect of the successful journey to recovery.

The reasons addicts relapse may include:

- That they haven't fully committed to the 12 Step program, and that they are only using it as a format that they have then redesigned to suit their own convenience. This is asking for trouble!
- That they are not prepared to make the spiritual journey that is required. A person can be spiritual without necessarily being religious.
- That they have not committed to abstinence, because for example, they believe their problem is with cocaine, and not with alcohol. WRONG!

It is to be hoped that after relapsing, the addict eventually realises that they can no longer go on as they have been. That they are ready for a change; that they are willing to try another way. – The only way -- TOTAL commitment to the 12 steps way.

12. Learn how to manage your relationship with your addict

We recognise that their behaviour seems senseless to those who don't suffer from addiction, in as much as it makes no sense to continue along the path of catastrophic self-destruction. Why would anyone continue to put their hand into a fire? The explanation is that addiction is a powerful force, immune to reason, and deaf to common sense. It is a parasite, consuming the individual's true self until nothing is left but the addict.

No matter what we say, no matter how we cajole, bully or plead, the addiction always comes first. It is a brutal master and a cruel tyrant that controls its victims. It is a terrifying psychological illness over which neither they nor you have control. The addict will always put their "substance" before their family. It is for this reason that we must devise a way to manage our addicts, so that they don't destroy us as collateral damage. In focussing on self-preservation, we cannot be found guilty of selfishness.

In Al-Anon, a support group that helps those who love people trapped in addiction, there is a saying: "Separate with love". Essentially, this means that we need to put our emotional health and happiness first, and not get sucked into the mess and drama that goes hand in hand with addiction. We need to separate, not out of anger or resentment, but because we need to stay sane. Addiction is not simply confined to those who are addicted; it spreads its tentacles to embrace everyone that it touches.

Separating with love doesn't mean turning your back on someone. It means detaching emotionally so that the addict's behaviour ceases to effect and destroy us, and we are able to communicate with them calmly and objectively. Only after we have dealt with our own emotions can we begin to offer compassion and support to others. You can have compassion for their illness, but it is essential to show compassion towards yourself as well.

It might be useful to look at the Al-Anon website.

The most important thing to understand is that we cannot change the behaviour of others. All we can do is change our response to it. Taking a step back emotionally is neither selfish nor unloving. On the contrary, it may help you to reopen communication and help your addict find the true road of recovery.

This section was taken from an article by Sally Brampton who herself is a recovering addict and therefore speaks with some qualification.

13. Remember that nobody chooses to be an addict, any more than they would choose to be diabetic, epileptic or physically disabled

I realise that I am repeating this refrain, but I do so without apology, because grasping this fundamental is essential for families who are being collaterally damaged by addiction.

14. Encourage them to begin a new lifestyle in a healthy environment

I suppose that most people would think that this is a matter of commonsense.

The probable starting point is to find a suitable job, so that a regular income can be secured.

It would make little sense for an alcoholic to decide to run a pub.

It would make little sense for a cocaine addict to decide to run a nightclub.

It has been suggested that a recovering addict should try to tick the following boxes regarding lifestyle:

- Have a job with a sensible routine.
- Have a job with sociable hours.

- Have a job that helps them to mix with decent people, who are not addicts.
- Be sure to ditch all the old "friends" who were part of their addiction scene.
- Have a job which builds self-confidence rather than challenge or destroy it. This doesn't necessarily need to be a job for life.
- Design exercise into the daily routine.
- Work on achieving regular and adequate sleep patterns. This will be helped by having suitable exercise.
- Consider developing the practice of meditation.
- Develop a passion for a pastime or hobby that involves the "whole being". This might be art, sport, music, collecting things or making things – as long as the individual finds the activity challenging or absorbing. This hobby is something that is done because of a desire to do it, rather than a need to do it. Hobbies often fulfil a more important role when employment gives limited job satisfaction.

15. Encourage them to consider Cognitive Behavioural Therapy (CBT) which they also need to pay for themselves if they have the resources. If they don't have the resources, the family or the state should play their role

Genetics seem to play a very important role in addiction, but not every person who has the genetic potential becomes dependent. Genes seem to be a necessary factor but not a sufficient and sole causal factor. Stress is public enemy No.1 in the brain of those who possess the genetic potential for addiction.

These causal factors are emotional, biological, cognitive, and spiritual. Without addressing these issues, there is no long term cure for addiction, and by cure, we mean re-establishing the focus of control in the neo-cortex and away from the needy, craving, compulsive, reptilian midbrain. This is what will make the difference between long-term sobriety, chronic relapse, and death for a chemically dependent person.

During the period that a person is an addict their patterns of thinking, feeling and behaving, can become seriously dysfunctional.

CBT is a form of talking therapy that aims to help change the way that the addict thinks, feels, and behaves. There are also some on-line sites that are credited with being most helpful.

It looks at how the addict can change any negative patterns of thinking and behaviour that may be causing difficulties. In turn, this can change the way they feel.

CBT theory suggests that it isn't events themselves that upset the addict, but the meaning they give to them.

Their dysfunctional thoughts can block them from seeing things that don't fit in with what they believe to be true. This problem can prevent them from learning anything new.

Re-establishing "normal" patterns of thinking, feeling and behaving, are an essential step on the road to recovery for an addict.

Never reject the use of a psychiatrist if this may speed recovery.

16. Persuade them to study The Art of Happiness by the Dalai Lama

The following observations by the Dalai Lama are helpful in the pursuit of happiness once the addict has made progress down the road of recovery. Also included are some observations by Professor Michael Argyle:

- The very purpose of our life is to seek happiness.

- Happiness cannot simply be bought by money and by a devotion to materialism.

- It is suggested that we should learn to get more out of everyday things, not want more than we need, and that we should take time to savour our special moments.

- We should explore spirituality in order to balance our materialism. Happiness is more likely to be achieved by having a spiritual dimension.

- Basic spirituality is needed to develop basic human qualities such as goodness, kindness, compassion, caring, empathy, tolerance and forgiveness. This spirituality is the development of the spirit and can be achieved without being involved with a specific brand of religion.

- The purpose of a religion is to make people happy, and to make the world a better place by providing a framework of ethical behaviour. It is therefore regrettable that religions can be so divisive and that so much of man's inhumanity to man is perpetrated in the name of religion.

- Happiness is a state of mind rather than the result of external events. These events can temporarily raise or lower our state of wellbeing, before it returns to its normal baseline. It's the baseline that's the important thing. This baseline is probably hard-wired into us at birth, but it can also be raised by our own efforts.

- If you are not happy, maybe you are pursuing the wrong objectives. These therefore need to be reappraised and reset.

- Happiness can be improved by frequently counting our blessings, and by recognising how fortunate we are compared with so many others.

- It is perhaps obvious that happiness is assisted by a calm mind, as opposed to one that is in a state of turmoil.

- Positive attitudes are helpful towards happiness, whereas negative attitudes are unhelpful. Consciously developing our more positive attitudes can act as an antidote to the harmful negative ones.

- Working on our mental outlook is a more effective means of achieving happiness than seeking it through external sources such as wealth, position or even physical health.

- There can easily be a conflict between happiness and pleasure. Many things that give you temporary pleasure, will not give you long term happiness e.g.: cocaine, excessive alcohol, violence, and many other pleasures of the flesh (like playing away).

- It is essential to develop positive attitudes, and to eliminate negative attitudes in order to create a mental state that will lead to happiness. Positive attitudes include kindness, empathy, warmth and compassion. Negative attitudes include hatred, jealousy and anger. These can consume you and destroy you.

- It is easier to be happy if you have good relations with people rather than bad ones. It therefore makes sense to focus on people's good points, and be merely aware of their bad points rather than have the negativity of solely focussing on them.

- It is clear that feelings of love, closeness, empathy and compassion, bring happiness. The opposites clearly bring unhappiness.

- Intimate relationships are essential for both mental and physical health. This intimacy may be either physical or non-physical. Being "connected" to people is important. Isolation is the damaging alternative.

- When relating to other people it is always useful to have an understanding of their backgrounds, because this may shape their behaviour towards you and the rest of the world. "Never judge a man until you have walked a mile in his shoes."

- We all have problems! Always remember that NO-ONE lives a life that is free of suffering and loss. It's part of life and is a punctuation in our happiness. Having no understanding of the natural and normal part that suffering plays in our lives, can lead to an unhelpful victim mentality.

- It is not helpful to continue to relive grievances of the past as this guarantees the continuation of unhappiness. After a period of time, it is essential to "move on".

- We all make mistakes and therefore feel both regret and guilt. It is important to experience these emotions, but equally important that we don't wallow in them. Unless we "move on" these negative emotions will cause us unhappiness.

- Our lives consist of continual change. We make ourselves unhappy if we fail to accept the natural and inevitable changes in life --- particularly those associated with the aging process, and those that occur during the evolution of a long relationship.

- Anger and hatred are like a fisherman's hook. It is very important for us to ensure that we are not caught up by this hook. These negative emotions can and usually do make us unhappy.

- Searching for balance is essential for one's physical, emotional, and spiritual growth. Extremes should be avoided, as should obsessiveness in any particular direction.

- Suffering can be a positive experience because it not only reduces arrogance, but helps empathy and compassion. "What doesn't destroy me makes me stronger"!!

- Being aware of the impermanence of our lives as expressed as "the 7 ages of man", we should apply some urgency to making positive use of every precious moment.

- All negative mental states act as obstacles to our happiness. Negative emotions include conceit, arrogance, jealousy, envy and lust, but the most damaging are anger and hatred. Having said this, even anger can be turned to advantage if for example it gives us the energy and motivation to attempt to "right" a social wrong or unfairness. The worst emotion is hatred as it has no other function than simply destroying us, both in the short-term and in the long-term. The only factor that can give us refuge from the destructive effects of anger and hatred are the development and use of tolerance and patience

- An end result or product of patience and tolerance is forgiveness. When you are truly patient and tolerant, then forgiveness comes naturally. We should not confuse these qualities with weakness.

- On anxiety. If there is a solution to a problem, there is no need to worry. If there is no solution to the problem, there is no sense in worrying either.

- A sincere and honest motivation will often remove any anxiety or self-consciousness.

- Honesty and self-confidence are closely linked. Being totally honest with yourself and others as to what you can and cannot do, helps to overcome a lack of self-confidence.

According to the observations of Professor Michael Argyle, there are four criteria that are hugely important in the successful pursuit of happiness (called subjective wellbeing by the scientists). They are practical measures and hold no contradictions to the observations of the Dalai Lama that are set out above.

1. To be truly happy one needs a fulfilling job which commands commitment and focus. This may well be helped by having a skill or a profession.

2. The key is to have a passion for a hobby or pastime that involves the "whole being". This might be art, sport, music, collecting things or making things—as long as the individual finds the activity challenging or absorbing. This hobby is something that is done because of a desire to do it, rather than a need to do it. Hobbies often fulfil a more important role when employment gives limited job satisfaction.

3. A happy relationship is a most reliable source of happiness. This is probably because we are a pair bonding species.

4. Living within one's means is an essential ingredient for happiness. This usually means developing the habit of spending from savings, rather than having a "live now pay later" attitude. Having a cash reserve for "a rainy day" seldom causes unhappiness!!

17. EPILOGUE. Be aware that despite their best efforts, a full recovery eludes some addicts. We as family, have to steel ourselves to the reality that continuing and chronic addiction often causes death

It is clearly stated in re-hab units that untreated chronic addicts will sadly have a final destination of either jail, institutions or death.

For proof of this, we only need to refer again to the sad death of Eva Rausing.

This lady had more financial resources than we can imagine, to buy the very best of treatment at any location in the world.

She had all the reasons in the world to fight for her recovery. She had every reason to want to live.

She had a loving relationship with her husband, and four children that she loved very much. Sadly drugs became a greater priority than these relationships.

Despite having an 11 year period when she was totally clean, she died in self-imposed squalor at the age of 48.

Another sad story to hit the headlines in 2014 was the death of Philip Seymour Hoffman, the critically acclaimed character actor. He died of heroin over dosage.

Hoffman had a history of excessive drug abuse in earlier life but sobered up and became clean when he was 22. He then kept clean of drink and drugs for the next 23 years. During that time he won an Oscar and became a father to 3 children. Then one day in 2012, he started taking opium based prescription painkillers known as opioids, and before long he was back on cocaine and heroin. Sadly, his experience – at least as far as narcotics go – is far from unusual.

The problem arises from the fact that prescription painkillers such as OxyContin and Vicodin, are chemically similar to heroin and therefore act as gateway drugs to heroin abuse. It would seem to be unbelievably irresponsible for doctors to prescribe these drugs to people with a history of abuse --- beware the doctor!!

It adds to the overall problem that heroin is now produced in a form that can be smoked or snorted as opposed to the unpleasantness and degradation of injection. Heroin has become the drug of choice in America and has superseded cocaine. Its use has spiked in the last few years and poses huge social problems.

The frequently quoted stats are that:

- 1 in 3 addicts get clean on the 1st attempt and then successfully manage their addiction.
- 1 in 3 get clean but then relapse before getting into a position where they can successfully manage their addiction.
- 1 in 3 never get clean and will therefore probably die as a result of their addiction.

These figures translate into the frightening fact that around 33 addicts in every 100 will never be successful in managing their addiction.

I personally know 6 addicts who have died as a result of their addiction.

As the old truism goes "We must hope for the best, but prepare for the worst"

Our love alone will not be enough to guarantee their survival...

As a postscript, for those who would like to learn more about this subject, it may be helpful to:

- Read *The Big Book*, which was written in 1939 for alcoholics, but created the format of the 12 steps which is used to help those with all manner of other addictions. This book has sold in excess of 30 million copies!! In 2011, Time magazine placed it on its list of the 100 best and most influential books written in the English language since the magazine began in 1923.

- Attend open meetings for non addicts at your local Alcoholics Anonymous (AA) or Narcotics Anonymous (NA).
- Attend a meeting at your local Al-Anon, which offers support to the families of addicts. Al-Anon can be most helpful to those families where different members are reacting differently to the addiction problem. Two parents may not view their child's addiction in the same way. One parent may not wish to discuss it at all. If this is the case, the parent who wishes to find out more about addiction should go to Al-Anon. It is common to go to these meetings and listen without sharing, until ready to do so. It may be a great release of stored up frustration and sometimes anger, which can both damage relationships inside the family. Those who want help should not hesitate to break ranks and get it. This is also an ideal forum for families to discuss such painful subjects as: addicts that are arrested for debts, the impact of criminal records on job seeking, and how to deal with the problem of your child "sleeping rough".

And as a final word, families generally, need to be reminded of the following observations regarding the nurturing/raising of their children and grandchildren:

- It is really important to establish the natural talents of a child as soon as possible, and then to nurture those talents. By developing the child's natural talents, you provide them with the confidence to take healthy risks, to push boundaries and to learn on their own. It is clearly better for a child to view themselves as a successful orator rather than a mediocre mathematician --- an inspiring creative artist rather than a failed sportsman.
- The foundation of self-esteem is assembled from the building blocks of childhood, with the strongest influence being the parents.
- In the debate of nature versus nurture, it could be said that nature gives the talents, but that nurture definitely develops them.
- In any event, parents should show love, compassion and tolerance for their child's weaknesses, and always strive to build them up.
- Structure and routine are essential for children in their everyday lives because it makes them feel secure. This does not mean a rigidity that excludes spontaneity. The truth is that children thrive on structure because it makes them feel safe, loved and cared for.
- If a child grows into an adult with a healthy spirit, a positive outlook, and a sense of personal accomplishment and importance, they

will be a better partner, friend and parent. It's not about being selfish, it's about being the best you can be, and rejecting those who keep you down. It's about taking responsibility for your own happiness. It's about living your life free of fear.

18. Horizon 5/02/08-- quoting a paper in the Lancet

The Premiere League of Dangerous Drugs, listed in order of danger, using the following criteria:

- Danger to the individual.
- Danger to Society.
- Addictive power.

1. Heroin

2. Cocaine & Crack

3. Barbiturates

4. Street Methadone

5. Alcohol

6. Ketamine

7. Benzodiazepines

8. Amphetamines

9. Tobacco – The most addictive

10. Buprenorphine

11. Cannabis

12. Solvents

13. 4MTA – Flatliner

14. LSD

15. Methyl Phenidate – Ritalin

16. Anabolic Steroids

17. GHB- Liquid Ecstasy

18. Ecstasy

19. Alkyl Nitrite

20. Khat